INITIAL
GUITAR

Published by
Trinity College London Press Ltd
trinitycollege.com

Registered in England
Company no. 09726123

Photography by Zute Lightfoot, lightfootphoto.com

Printed in England by Caligraving Ltd

Parental and Teacher Guidance:

The songs in Trinity's Rock & Pop syllabus have been arranged
to represent the artists' original recordings as closely and
authentically as possible. Popular music frequently deals with
subject matter that some may find offensive or challenging.
It is possible that the songs may include material that some
might find unsuitable for use with younger learners.

We recommend that parents and teachers exercise their own
judgement to satisfy themselves that the lyrics of selected
songs are appropriate for the students concerned. As you
will be aware, there is no requirement that all songs in this
syllabus must be learned. Trinity does not associate itself with,
adopt or endorse any of the opinions or views expressed in
the selected songs.

THE EXAM AT A GLANCE

In your exam you will perform a set of three songs and one of the session skills assessments. You can choose the order of your set list.

SONG 1

Choose a song from this book.

SONG 2

Choose *either* a different song from this book
or a song from the list of additional Trinity Rock & Pop arrangements, available at trinityrock.com
or a song you have chosen yourself: this could be your own cover version or a song that you have written. It should be at the same level as the songs in this book and match the parameters at trinityrock.com

SONG 3: TECHNICAL FOCUS

Song 3 is designed to help you develop specific and relevant techniques in performance. Choose one of the technical focus songs from this book, which cover two specific technical elements.

SESSION SKILLS

Choose *either* **playback** *or* **improvising**.

Session skills are an essential part of every Rock & Pop exam. They are designed to help you develop the techniques music industry performers need.

Sample tests are available in our *Session Skills* books and free examples can be downloaded from trinityrock.com

ACCESS ALL AREAS

GET THE FULL ROCK & POP EXPERIENCE ONLINE AT TRINITYROCK.COM

We have created a range of digital resources to support your learning and give you insider information from the music industry, available online.
You will find support, advice and digital content on:

- Songs, performance and technique
- Session skills
- The music industry

You can access tips and tricks from industry professionals featuring:

- Bite-sized videos that include tips from professional musicians on techniques used in the songs
- 'Producer's notes' on the tracks, to increase your knowledge of rock and pop
- Blog posts on performance tips, musical styles, developing technique and advice from the music industry

JOIN US ONLINE AT:

 /TRINITYROCKANDPOP    @TRINITY_ROCK    /TRINITYROCKANDPOP   and at **TRINITYROCK.COM**

CONTENTS

THE AUDIO

Professional demo & backing tracks can be downloaded free, see inside cover for details.

Music preparation and book layout by Andrew Skirrow for Camden Music Services
Music consultants: Nick Crispin, Chris Walters, Christopher Hussey, Anders Rye
Audio arranged, recorded & produced by Tom Fleming
Guitar arrangements by Tom Fleming

Musicians
Bass: Tom Fleming
Drums: George Double
Guitar: Tom Fleming
Sax: Derek Nash
Vocals: Bo Walton, Alison Symons

YOUR
PAGE
NOTES

TECHNICAL FOCUS

20TH CENTURY BOY
T REX

WORDS AND MUSIC: MARC BOLAN

SINGLE BY
T Rex

B-SIDE
Free Angel

RELEASED
March 1973

RECORDED
**3 December, 1972
Toshiba Recording
Studios, Tokyo, Japan**

LABEL
EMI

WRITER
Marc Bolan

PRODUCER
Tony Visconti

T Rex originally started as 60s folk duo Tyrannosaurus Rex until frontman and songwriter Marc Bolan switched from acoustic to electric guitar and shortened the band's name. With a new sound for the 70s, Bolan quickly became both a pop star and a pioneer of the glam rock phenomenon.

'20th Century Boy' was released in March 1973 as a non-album single and reached No. 3 on the UK singles chart. It was the band's tenth top-ten hit (four of them No. 1s) and was produced by Tony Visconti, who produced the band's first nine albums between 1968 and 1974. The song became a hit again in 1993, peaking at No. 13 following its use in a Levi's jeans advert starring Brad Pitt. David Bowie, an old friend of Bolan's who performed with him a week before Bolan's tragic death in a car crash, memorably duetted with English rock band Placebo in a live version of '20th Century Boy' at the 1999 Brit Awards.

TECHNICAL FOCUS

Two technical focus elements are featured in this song:

- Rhythm of the riff
- Power chords

This song starts with a well-known riff, so make sure the rhythm of the riff is completely accurate. After the riff, the verse begins with some power chords. Take care to play these cleanly with only the notes that are written.

20TH CENTURY BOY

WORDS AND MUSIC: MARC BOLAN

Intro

Rock ♩ = 130 (2 bars count-in)

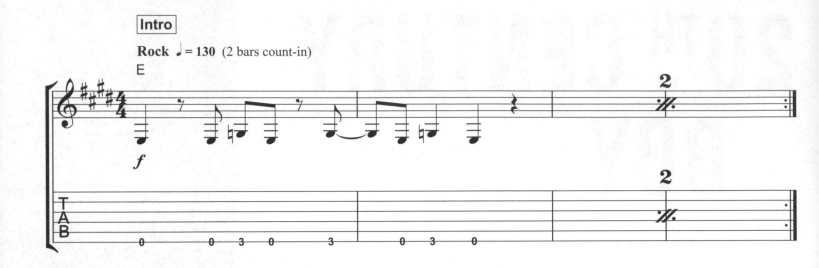

Verse

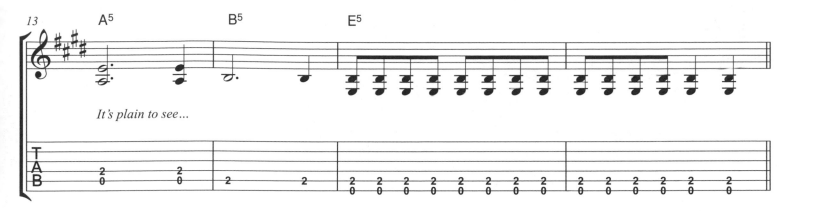

It's plain to see...

Chorus

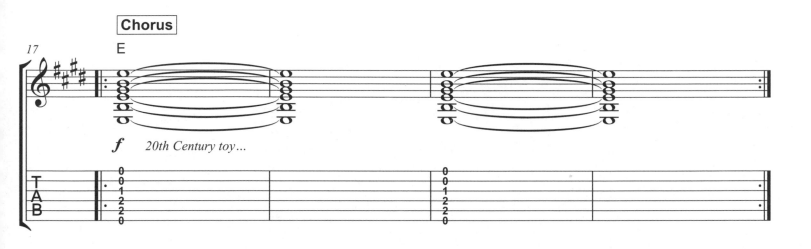

f   *20th Century toy...*

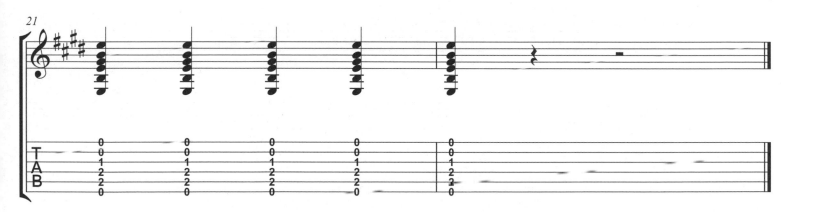

YOUR
PAGE
NOTES

LILY WAS HERE
DAVID A STEWART, FEAT. CANDY DULFER

SINGLE BY
David A Stewart

ALBUM
Lily Was Here

RELEASED
**November 1989
(Netherlands)
12 February 1990
(UK)**

RECORDED
1989

LABEL
Anxious

WRITER
David A Stewart

PRODUCER
David A Stewart

WORDS AND MUSIC: DAVID A STEWART

David A Stewart is an English musician, songwriter and producer who achieved global success in the 1980s as one half of Eurythmics with Annie Lennox. Stewart co-wrote and produced all of the duo's material, including the hits 'Sweet Dreams (Are Made of This)', 'Who's That Girl?', 'Here Comes the Rain Again' and 'There Must Be an Angel (Playing with My Heart)'.

'Lily Was Here' was written for the soundtrack to the 1989 Dutch film *De Kassière*. The soundtrack album, also entitled *Lily Was Here* after the film's international title, became Stewart's first solo album. It was released within months of Eurythmics' *We Too Are One*, the pair's final album before a ten-year break. 'Lily Was Here' spent five weeks at No. 1 in the Netherlands, prompting it to be released as a single internationally and becoming a sizeable hit worldwide. The track marked the recording debut of Dutch saxophonist Candy Dulfer, who launched a solo career on the back of the track's success and would go on to perform with Prince, Pink Floyd and Van Morrison.

⚡ **PERFORMANCE TIPS**

In this song you take a lead role, alternating with the solo sax. When playing the melody, keep the notes even and the sound clean, and try not to let open strings ring on.

LILY WAS HERE

WORDS AND MUSIC: DAVID A STEWART

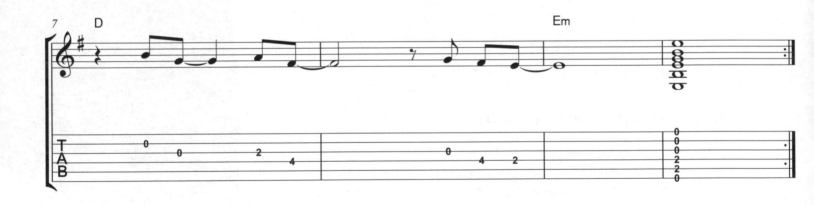

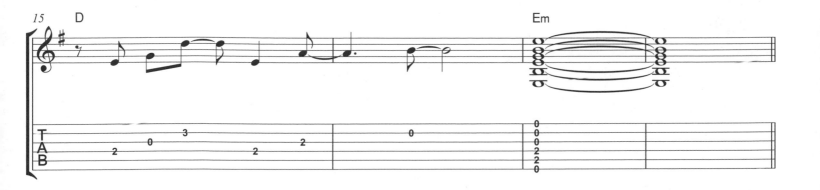

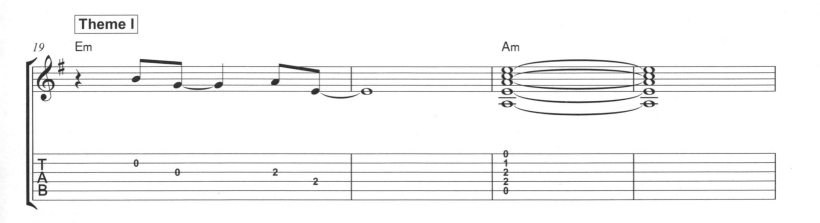

Theme I

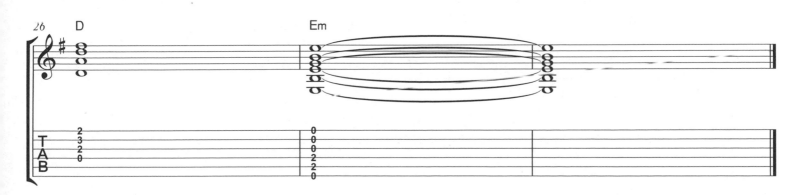

YOUR
PAGE
NOTES

TECHNICAL FOCUS

HOLE IN MY SHOE
TRAFFIC

WORDS AND MUSIC: DAVE MASON

SINGLE BY
Traffic

B-SIDE
Smiling Phases

RELEASED
August 1967

LABEL
Island
United Artists

WRITER
Dave Mason

PRODUCER
Jimmy Miller

A former frontman of the Spencer Davis Group, Steve Winwood left that hugely successful band in 1967 to form the group Traffic with Jim Capaldi (drums), Dave Mason (guitar) and Chris Wood (flute and saxophone). All six of the band's studio albums made the top 10 in either the UK or US before the band broke up in 1975.

'Hole in My Shoe' was written by Dave Mason, who also played sitar on this psychedelic pop classic. It was the group's biggest hit, reaching No. 2 in the UK in October 1967. Mason quit the band shortly after the song's success and before the release of Traffic's debut album *Dear Mr Fantasy*. He briefly rejoined in 1968 for the band's self-titled second album, the same year that Winwood, Wood and Mason appeared on The Jimi Hendrix Experience's *Electric Ladyland* album, with Mason playing acoustic 12-string guitar on 'All Along the Watchtower'. A version of 'Hole in My Shoe' was later released by the actor Nigel Planer, in character as the pacifist pessimist Neil from the BBC sitcom *The Young Ones*.

TECHNICAL FOCUS

Two technical focus elements are featured in this song:

- Balance
- Syncopation

You have two roles in this song: supporting at the start, and taking the lead from bar 14 onwards. Adjust your **balance** between these two styles: softer when you are accompanying and louder when you are soloing. When playing the solo, take care to be accurate with the **syncopation** in the melody.

HOLE IN MY SHOE

WORDS AND MUSIC: DAVE MASON

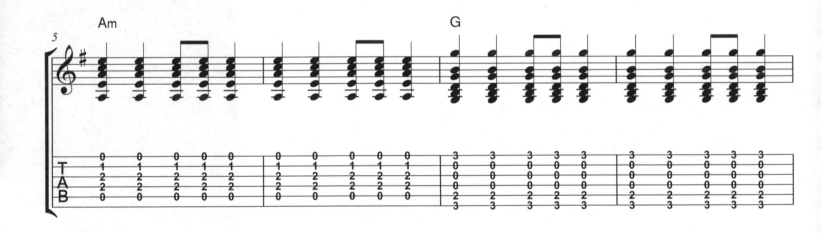

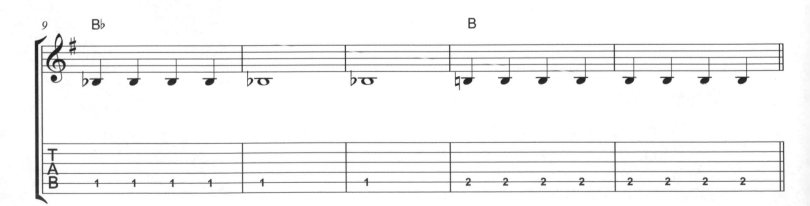

Verse 2

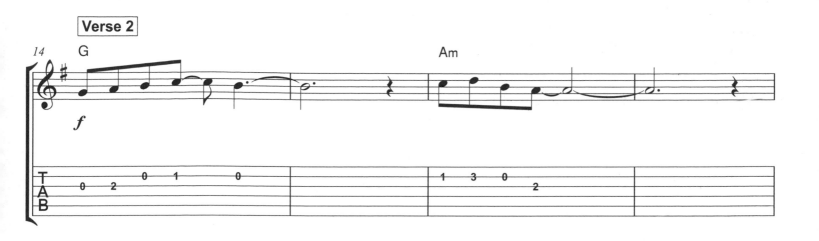

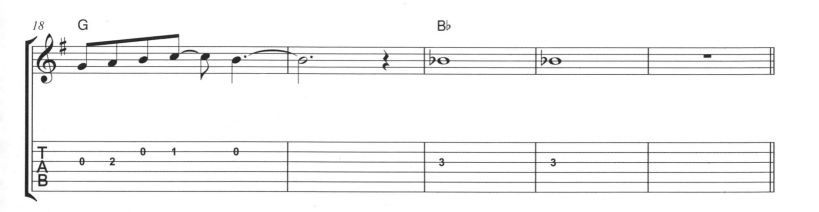

Instrumental

YOUR
PAGE
NOTES

MOUNTAIN AT MY GATES

FOALS

WORDS AND MUSIC: FOALS

SINGLE BY
Foals

ALBUM
What Went Down

RELEASED
21 July 2015

RECORDED
**2014–2015
La Fabrique Studios
Saint-Rémy-de-Provence
France (album)**

LABEL
**Transgressive
Warner Bros.**

WRITER
Foals

PRODUCER
James Ford

Foals are an English rock quintet formed in Oxford in 2005, fronted by singer and guitarist Yannis Philippakis. Over the course of four top-ten albums, two of them Mercury-nominated, they have become one of the UK's biggest bands, picking up Q Awards for Best Live Act in 2013 and Best Act in the World Today in 2015.

'Mountain at My Gates' was released as a single in July 2015, a month before the release of Foals' fourth studio album *What Went Down*. Working with Arctic Monkeys producer James Ford for the first time, the album revealed a much heavier and more riff-based sound compared to their previous indie dance and rock influenced material. 'Mountain at My Gates' is the second track on the album and topped the Billboard Alternative Songs chart in the US. The band performed the song on the long-running BBC live music TV series *Later with Jools Holland* in September 2015, almost eight years after their first appearance on the show.

⚡ PERFORMANCE TIPS

This song requires clean and accurate picking and clean chords at the bridge with no unwanted strings sounding. Look out also for the quieter dynamic at the bridge.

MOUNTAIN AT MY GATES

WORDS AND MUSIC: *FOALS*

Intro

Indie Rock ♩ = **104** (2 bars count-in)

Verse

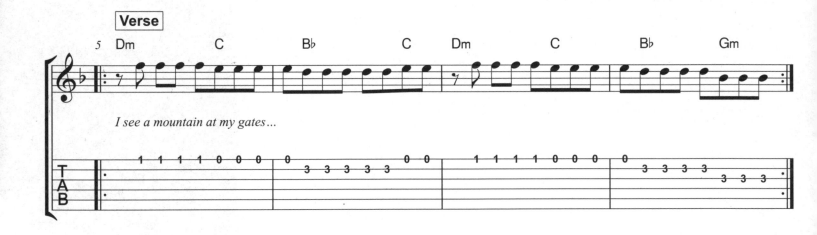

I see a mountain at my gates...

Chorus

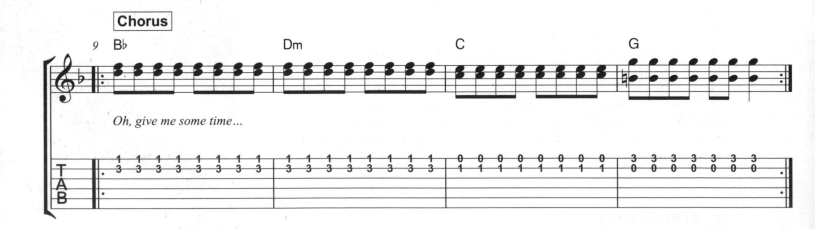

Oh, give me some time...

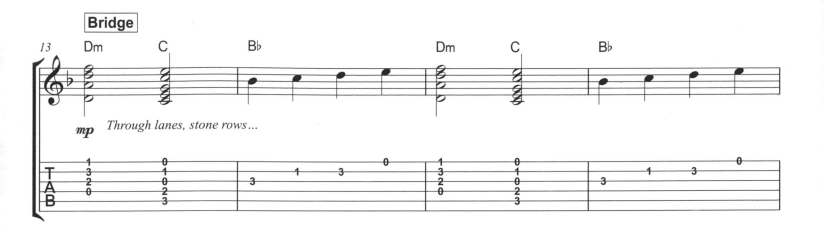

Through lanes, stone rows…

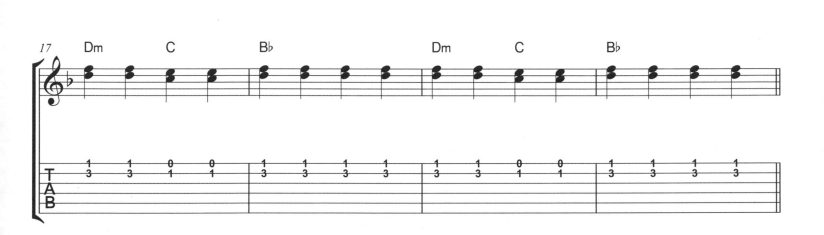

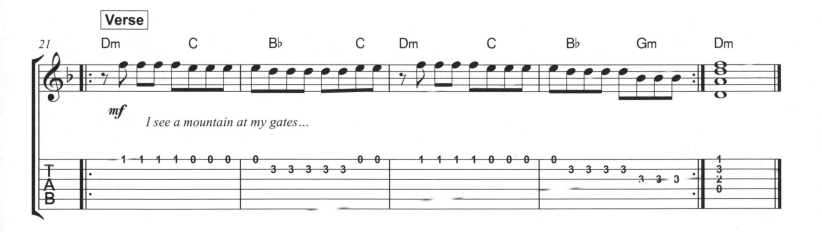

I see a mountain at my gates…

YOUR
PAGE
NOTES

ORANGE CRUSH

REM

WORDS AND MUSIC: BILL BERRY, PETER BUCK, MIKE MILLS MICHAEL STIPE

SINGLE BY
REM

ALBUM
Green

B-SIDE
**Ghost Riders
Dark Globe
Memphis Train Blues**

RELEASED
**7 November 1988 (album)
December 1988 (single)**

RECORDED
**May-September 1988
Ardent Studios
Memphis, Tennessee, USA**

**Bearsville Studios
Woodstock, New York,
USA (album)**

LABEL
Warner Bros.

WRITERS
**Bill Berry, Peter Buck
Mike Mills, Michael Stipe**

PRODUCERS
**Scott Litt
REM**

Formed in 1980 in Athens, Georgia, USA, REM are one of the most widely respected and commercially successful bands of the 80s, 90s and 00s. Comprising Michael Stipe (vocals), Peter Buck (guitars), Mike Mills (bass) and Bill Berry (drums), they released 15 studio albums between 1983 and 2011.

'Orange Crush' was the first single to be released from REM's major label debut, 1988's *Green* (Warner Bros), following five critically acclaimed albums released via independent label I.R.S. Records. In the liner notes to REM's 2011 career retrospective compilation album *Part Lies, Part Heart, Part Truth, Part Garbage 1982-2011*, Stipe wrote of 'Orange Crush that the song was 'a composite and fictional narrative in the first person, drawn from different stories I heard growing up around army bases. This song is about the Vietnam War and the impact on soldiers returning to a country that wrongly blamed them for the war.' (Stipe's father had served in Vietnam in the helicopter corps.) Both the single and the album *Green* helped establish the band's steadily building reputation as one of the world's biggest bands - something they would cement with their next album, *Out of Time*.

⚡ PERFORMANCE TIPS

This song requires some careful counting – at the start to make sure that each chord comes exactly on the first beat of the bar, and in the instrumental where syncopated rhythms appear. Clean picking is required to make sure that no extra strings sound when playing two- and three-note chords.

ORANGE CRUSH

WORDS AND MUSIC:
BILL BERRY, PETER BUCK,
MIKE MILLS, MICHAEL STIPE

Intro

Indie ♩ = 120
(2 bars count-in)

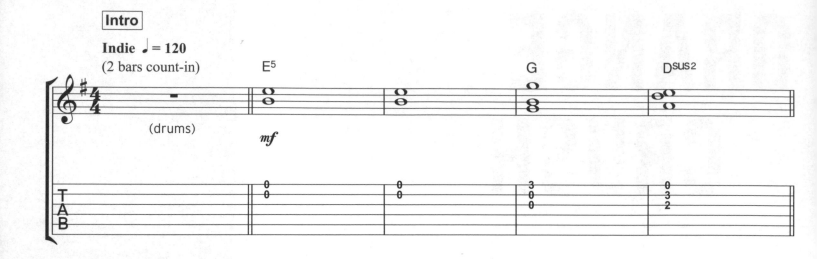

Verse

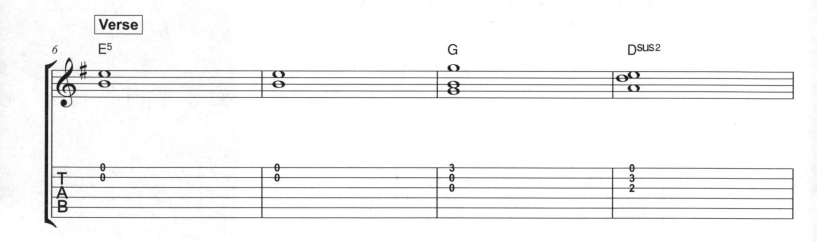

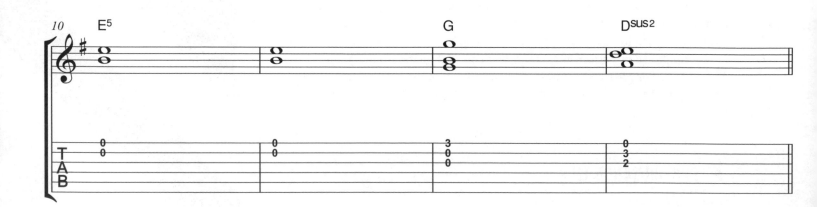

Instrumental

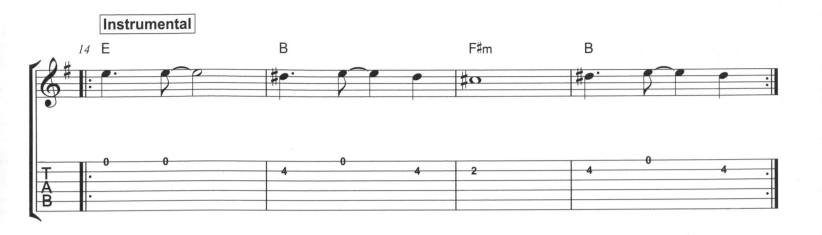

Verse

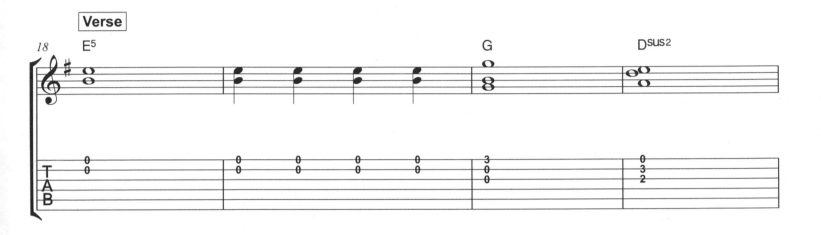

Instrumental

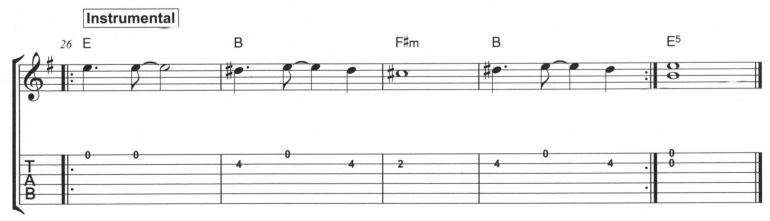

YOUR
PAGE
NOTES

RUNAWAY TRAIN
SOUL ASYLUM

WORDS AND MUSIC: DAVE PIRNER

SINGLE BY
Soul Asylum

ALBUM
Grave Dancers Union

B-SIDE
Black Gold (live)
Never Really Been (live)

RELEASED
6 October 1992 (album)
1 June 1993 (single)

RECORDED
May 1992
The Power Station, New York City, New York, USA

River Sound, New York City, New York, USA

Pachyderm Discs, Cannon Falls, Minnesota, USA

Cherokee Studios Hollywood, California USA (album)

LABEL
Columbia

WRITER
Dave Pirner

PRODUCER
Michael Beinhorn

American rock band Soul Asylum formed in Minneapolis, Minnesota in 1981, originally under the name Loud Fast Rules. The band comprised drummer Dave Pirner (later to become lead singer and guitarist), guitarist Dan Murphy and bassist Karl Mueller.

Soul Asylum had released five albums to little success prior to 1992's commercial breakthrough *Grave Dancers Union*, their first for Columbia Records after splitting with A&M. Released as the album's third single eight months later, 'Runaway Train' was the song that really changed the band's fortunes after reaching No. 5 in the US and No. 7 in the UK. Produced by Michael Beinhorn, whose other 90s productions include Soundgarden's *Superunknown* and Hole's *Celebrity Skin*, and featuring Booker T Jones on organ, it won the Grammy Award for Best Rock Song in 1994. The memorable accompanying video featured photographs and names of missing children from each country where it screened, and its wide exposure led to 26 children from around the world being found.

⚡ PERFORMANCE TIPS

This song is a test of clean chords. Some of the chords use all six strings but others don't, so take care not to let any unwanted strings sound. The louder pre-chorus features a syncopated rhythm which will require care.

RUNAWAY TRAIN

WORDS AND MUSIC: DAVE PIRNER

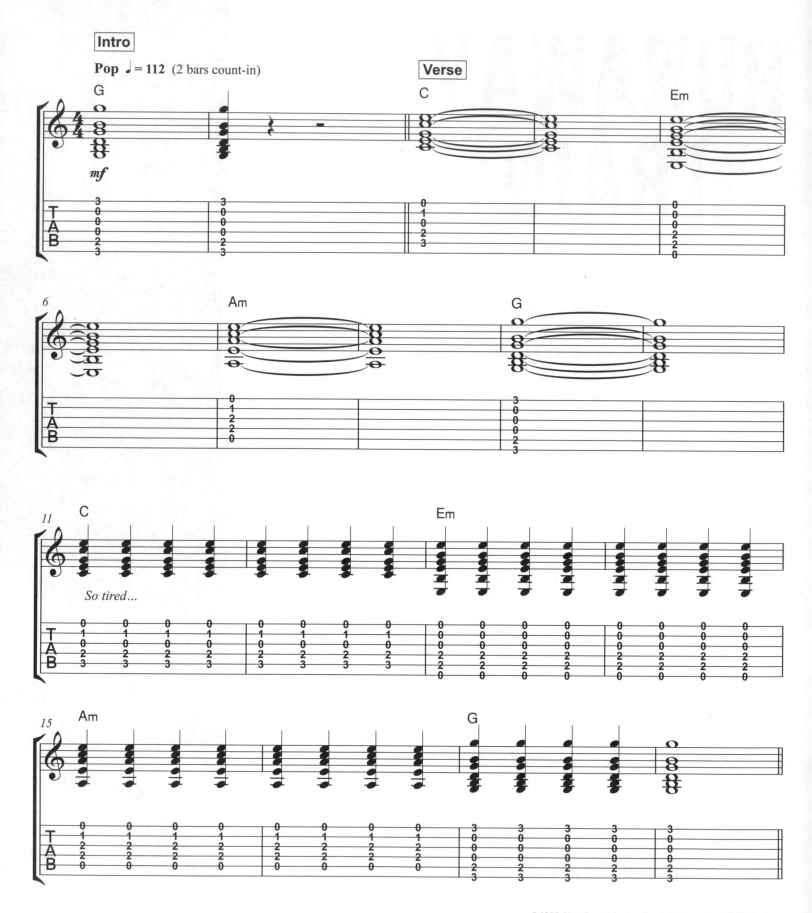

So tired...

Pre-chorus

Seems no one can help me now...

Chorus

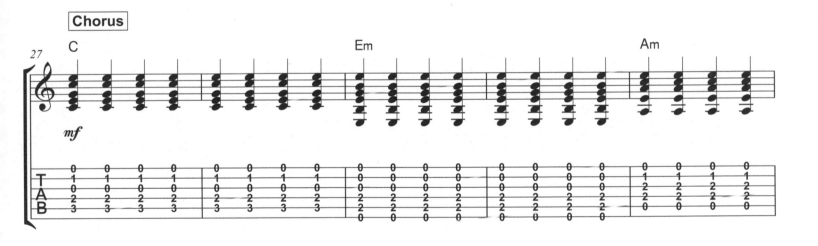

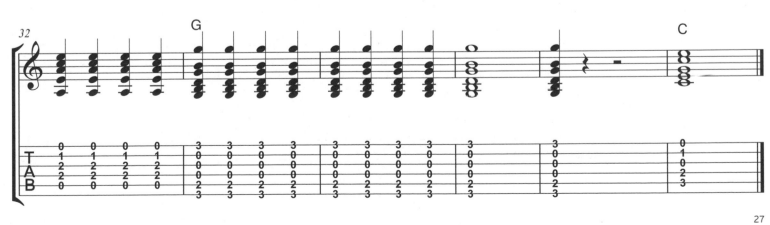

YOUR
PAGE
NOTES

TECHNICAL FOCUS

WHERE DID YOU SLEEP LAST NIGHT NIRVANA

WORDS AND MUSIC: TRADITIONAL, ARRANGED BY LEAD BELLY

SINGLE BY
Nirvana

ALBUM
MTV Unplugged in New York

RELEASED
1 November 1994

RECORDED
**18 November 1993
Sony Music Studios
New York City, New York
USA**

LABEL
DGC Records

WRITER
**Traditional
arranged by Lead Belly**

PRODUCERS
**Alex Coletti
Scott Litt
Nirvana**

Formed in Aberdeen, Washington, USA at the end of 1987, Nirvana had a massive cultural impact and huge commercial success with their second album *Nevermind* in 1991. Their line-up by this point comprised singer, guitarist and songwriter Kurt Cobain, bassist Krist Novoselic and drummer Dave Grohl.

Nirvana's haunting version of the 19th-century American folk song 'Where Did You Sleep Last Night' formed the climax of their MTV Unplugged in New York performance. Cobain was introduced to the song by Mark Lanegan, who recorded a version on his 1990 solo debut album on which Cobain played guitar and sang backing vocals. Lanegan discovered the song through American folk and blues musician Huddie 'Lead Belly' Ledbetter, who recorded several versions of the song in the 1940s. The band recorded their legendary acoustic set for MTV on 18 November 1993, six months before Cobain's tragic suicide. Released almost a year after it was recorded, the album was a huge success that hit No. 1 on both the US and UK album charts.

TECHNICAL FOCUS

Two technical focus elements are featured in this song:

- Melodic playing
- Chord accuracy

This song beings with some **melodic playing** for guitar, a passage that comes back later an octave higher. Play this with a sense of phrasing and make all notes clean and even. Later there is some **chord accuracy** to be aware of as you switch between two-note power chords and full chords with four, five and six strings. Be careful not to let any unwanted strings sound in these chordal passages.

WHERE DID YOU SLEEP LAST NIGHT

WORDS AND MUSIC: TRADITIONAL
ARRANGED BY LEAD BELLY

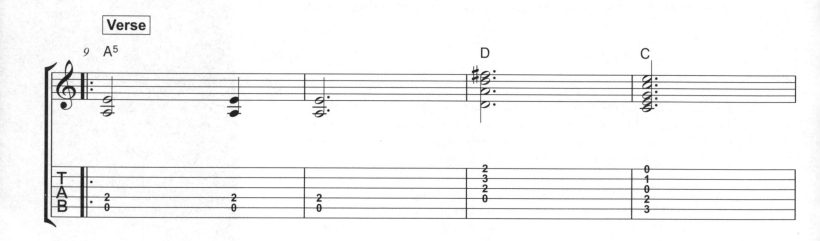

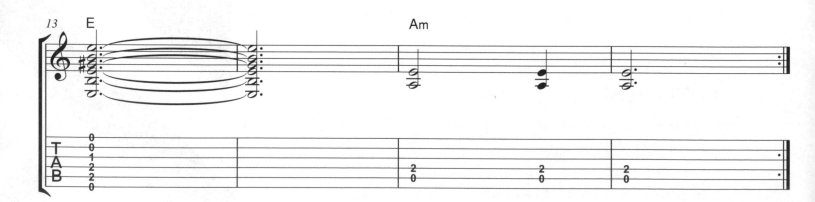

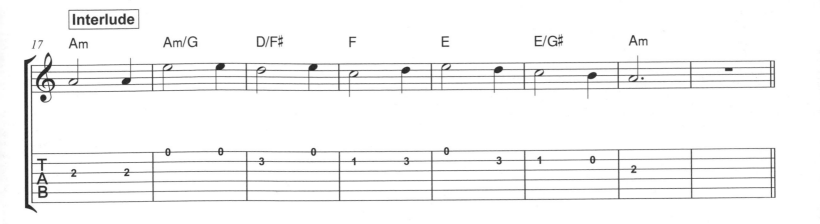

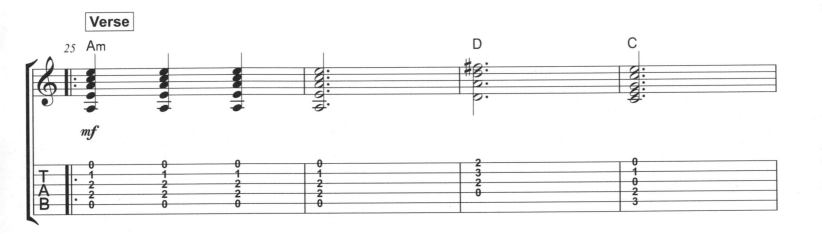

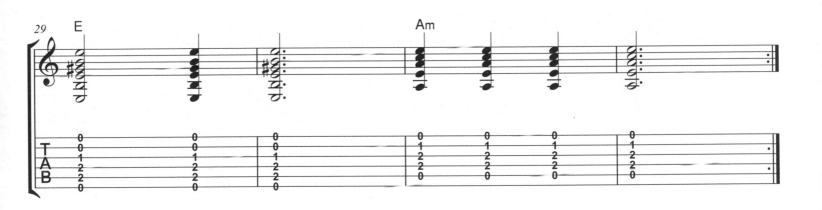

YOUR
PAGE
NOTES

WICKED GAME
CHRIS ISAAK

WORDS AND MUSIC: CHRIS ISAAK

SINGLE BY
Chris Isaak

ALBUM
Heart Shaped World

B-SIDE
**Wicked Game
(instrumental)**

RELEASED
**15 June 1989 (album)
8 November 1990 (single)**

RECORDED
**1988 Fantasy Studios
San Francisco, California
USA**

**Dave Wellhausen Studios
San Francisco, California
USA (album)**

LABEL
Reprise

WRITER
Chris Isaak

PRODUCER
Erik Jacobsen

Chris Isaak is a Californian singer-songwriter who emerged in the mid-80s but whose style, sound and influences came from 50s country blues, the rock'n'roll output of early Elvis Presley and the emotive, soaring croon of peak-era Roy Orbison.

'Wicked Game' was originally an album track on Isaak's third LP, 1989's *Heart Shaped World*. Cult film director David Lynch was a fan and used a number of tracks from the album for the soundtrack to his 1990 film *Wild at Heart*, including an instrumental version of 'Wicked Game'. After a radio programmer in Atlanta began playing the original vocal version, the positive response led to it being released as a single. Eventually it became a top-ten hit in both the UK and the US. Isaak wrote the song, but the distinctive lead guitar part was played by James Calvin Wilsey on a 1965 Fender Stratocaster, using reverb, delay and vibrato to enhance the ballad's melancholy mood.

⚡ PERFORMANCE TIPS

This song features a syncopated strumming rhythm as well as a syncopated rhythmic element in the melodic material at the intro and outro. Count these syncopations carefully. You'll also need to play the chords cleanly in the chorus and avoid extra strings sounding.

WICKED GAME

WORDS AND MUSIC: CHRIS ISAAK

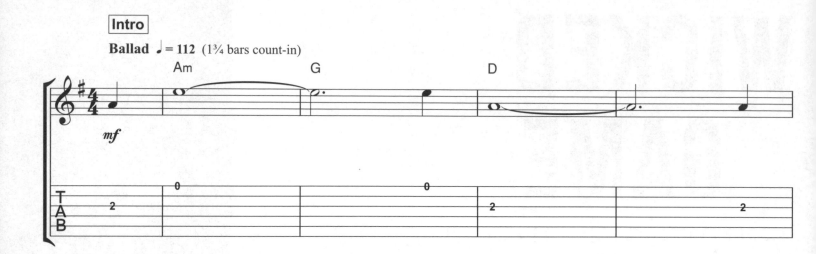

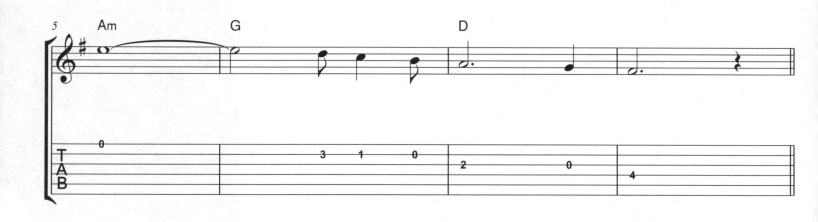

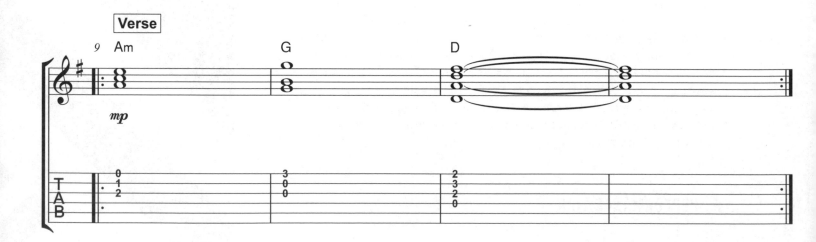

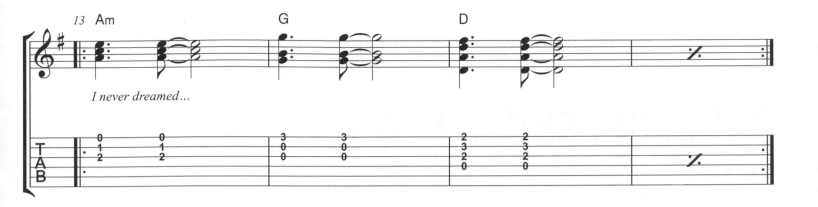

I never dreamed…

Chorus

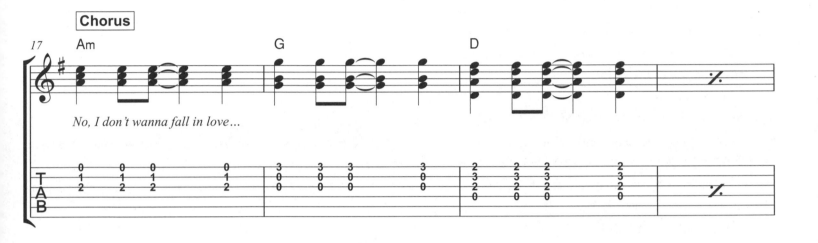

No, I don't wanna fall in love…

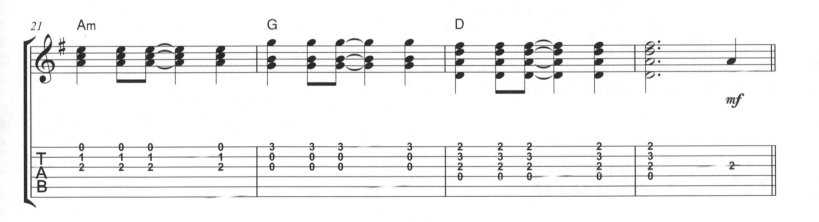

Outro

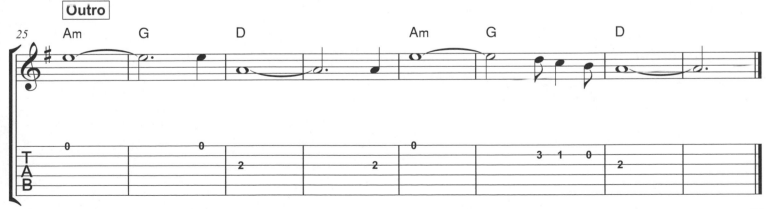

CHOOSING SONGS FOR YOUR EXAM

SONG 1

Choose a song from this book.

SONG 2

Choose a song which is:

Either a different song from this book

or from the list of additional Trinity Rock & Pop arrangements, available at trinityrock.com

or from a printed or online source

or your own arrangement

or a song that you have written yourself

You can play Song 2 unaccompanied or with a backing track (minus the guitar part). If you like, you can create a backing track yourself (or with friends), add your own vocals, or be accompanied live by another musician.

The level of difficulty and length of the song should be similar to the songs in this book and match the parameters available at trinityrock.com

When choosing a song, think about:

- Does it work on my instrument?

- Are there any technical elements that are too difficult for me? (If so, perhaps save it for when you do the next grade)

- Do I enjoy playing it?

- Does it work with my other songs to create a good set list?

SONG 3: TECHNICAL FOCUS

Song 3 is designed to help you develop specific and relevant techniques in performance. Choose one of the technical focus songs from this book, which cover two specific technical elements.

SHEET MUSIC

If your choice for Song 2 is not from this book, you must provide the examiner with a photocopy. The title, writers of the song and your name should be on the sheet music. You must also bring an original copy of the book, or a download version with proof of purchase, for each song that you perform in the exam.

Your music can be:

- A lead sheet with lyrics, chords and melody line

- A chord chart with lyrics

- A full score using conventional staff notation

PLAYING WITH BACKING TRACKS

All your backing tracks can be downloaded from soundwise.co.uk

- The backing tracks begin with a click track, which sets the tempo and helps you start accurately

- Be careful to balance the volume of the backing track against your instrument

- Listen carefully to the backing track to ensure that you are playing in time

If you are creating your own backing track, here are some further tips:

- Make sure that the sound quality is of a good standard

- Think carefully about the instruments/sounds you are using on the backing track

- Avoid copying what you are playing in the exam on the backing track – it should support, not duplicate

- Do you need to include a click track at the beginning?

COPYRIGHT IN A SONG

If you are a singer, instrumentalist or songwriter it is important to know about copyright. When someone writes a song they automatically own the copyright (sometimes called 'the rights'). Copyright begins once a piece of music has been documented or recorded (eg by video, CD or score notation) and protects the interests of the creators. This means that others cannot copy it, sell it, make it available online or record it without the owner's permission or the appropriate licence.

COVER VERSIONS

- When an artist creates a new version of a song it is called a 'cover version'

- The majority of songwriters subscribe to licensing agencies, also known as 'collecting societies'. When a songwriter is a member of such an agency, the performing rights to their material are transferred to the agency (this includes cover versions of their songs)

- The agency works on the writer's behalf by issuing licences to performance venues, who report what songs have been played, which in turn means that the songwriter will receive a payment for any songs used

- You can create a cover version of a song and use it in an exam without needing a licence

There are different rules for broadcasting (eg TV, radio, internet), selling or copying (pressing CDs, DVDs etc), and for printed material, and the appropriate licences should be sought out.

YOUR
PAGE
NOTES

YOUR
PAGE
NOTES

YOUR
PAGE
NOTES